Being Asian American

by Dr Raj
illustrated by Jean McMullen

Being Asian American by Dr. Raj

Copyright © 2024 by Rajendra S. Apte, MD, PhD

ISBNs
Hardcover: 979-8-9913830-0-4
Paperback: 979-8-9913830-1-1

All rights reserved. No portion of this book may be reproduced in any form without permission from the publisher, except as permitted by U.S. copyright law.

Watercolor Illustrations by Jean McMullen:
www.jmcmullenart.com

Cover and Interior Design by Carolyn Vaughan:
cvaughandesigns@gmail.com

Printed in the United States.

Dedicated to

Sherine, Aidin and Evan

I am Asian

I am American

I am me!

Don't box me

Don't cage me

I am not a model minority

I am me!

I am Indian

I am Iraqi

I am Chinese

I am Malaysian

And everything in between.

I am Asian

I am American

Let me be free!

Let me be me

Let me fly

Because I am me.

We are One but Many

Each Unique

A Diverse Tapestry

With some Shared Beliefs.

We are not a Monolith

But steeped in Cultures

Rich and Unique.

I am Jain and Sikh

I am Daoist and Shinto

I can be of Little Faith

But I have Faith in Me!

I am Asian

I am Hindu and Buddhist

I am Christian and Muslim

I am Jewish and Parsi.

I am Everything

I am nothing

I can be strong

But sometimes weak.

Don't box me

Don't cage me

Because I am me!

I am Asian

I am American

I am me!

I am an athlete

I am a student

I am a musician

I am an actor.

Sometimes I am good

And sometimes I am not

But I have passion

That will set me free.

With Pride in my heritage

And proud to be American

Unique not stereotyped

I am me!

I will break the glass ceiling

With or without you

So

Let me be me!

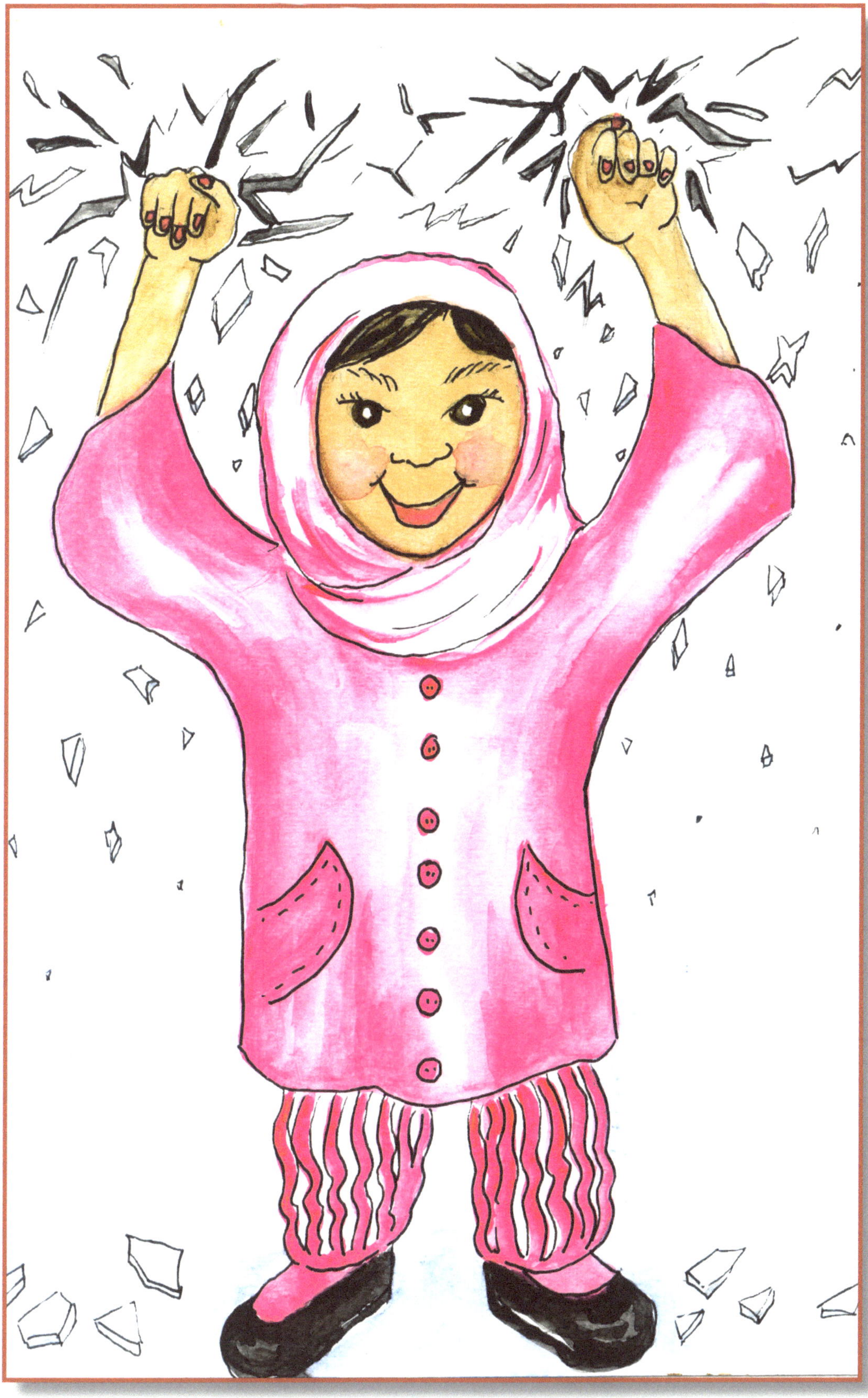

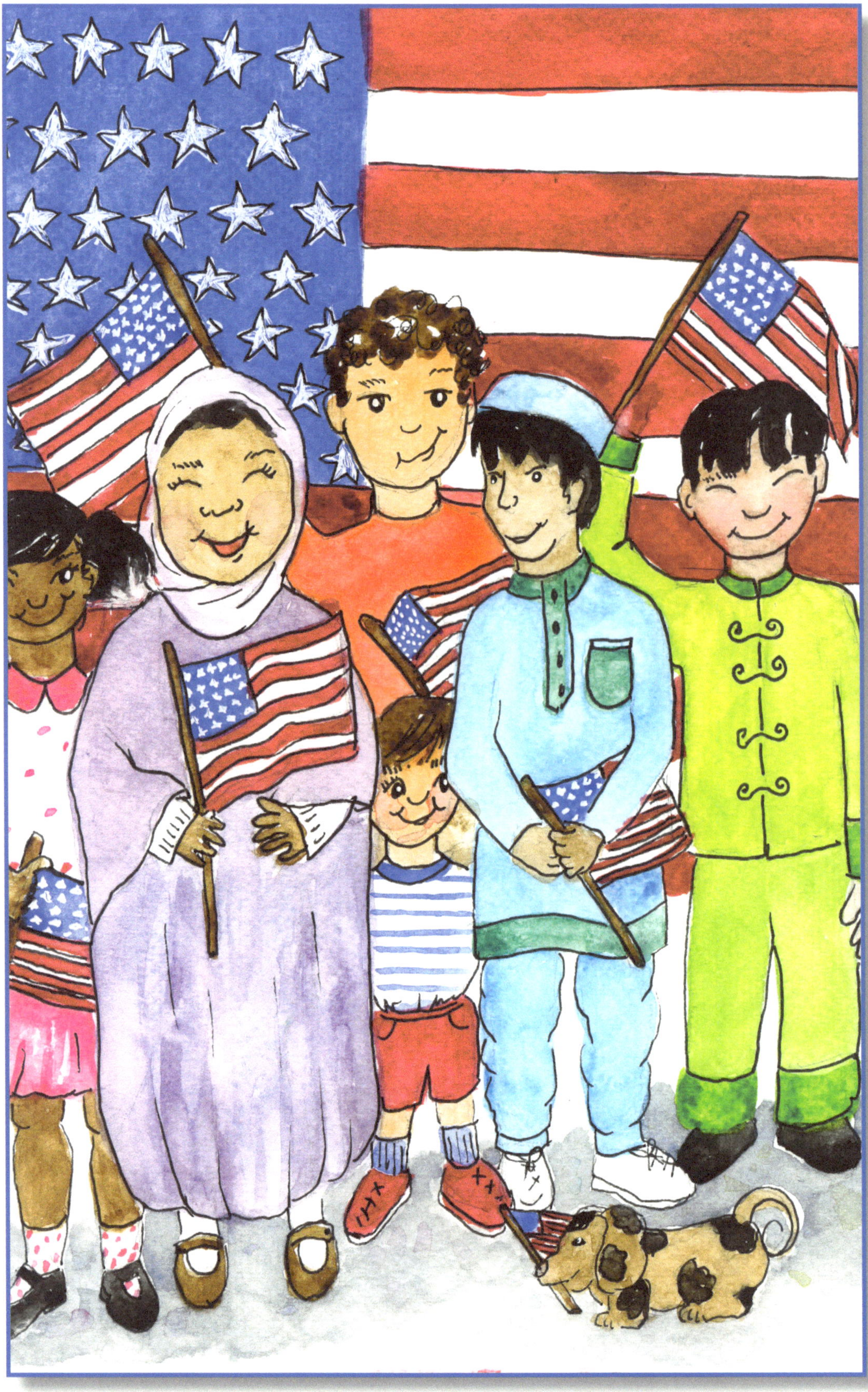

I am Asian

And American

I am everything I can be!

Don't box me

Don't cage me

Just let me be me!

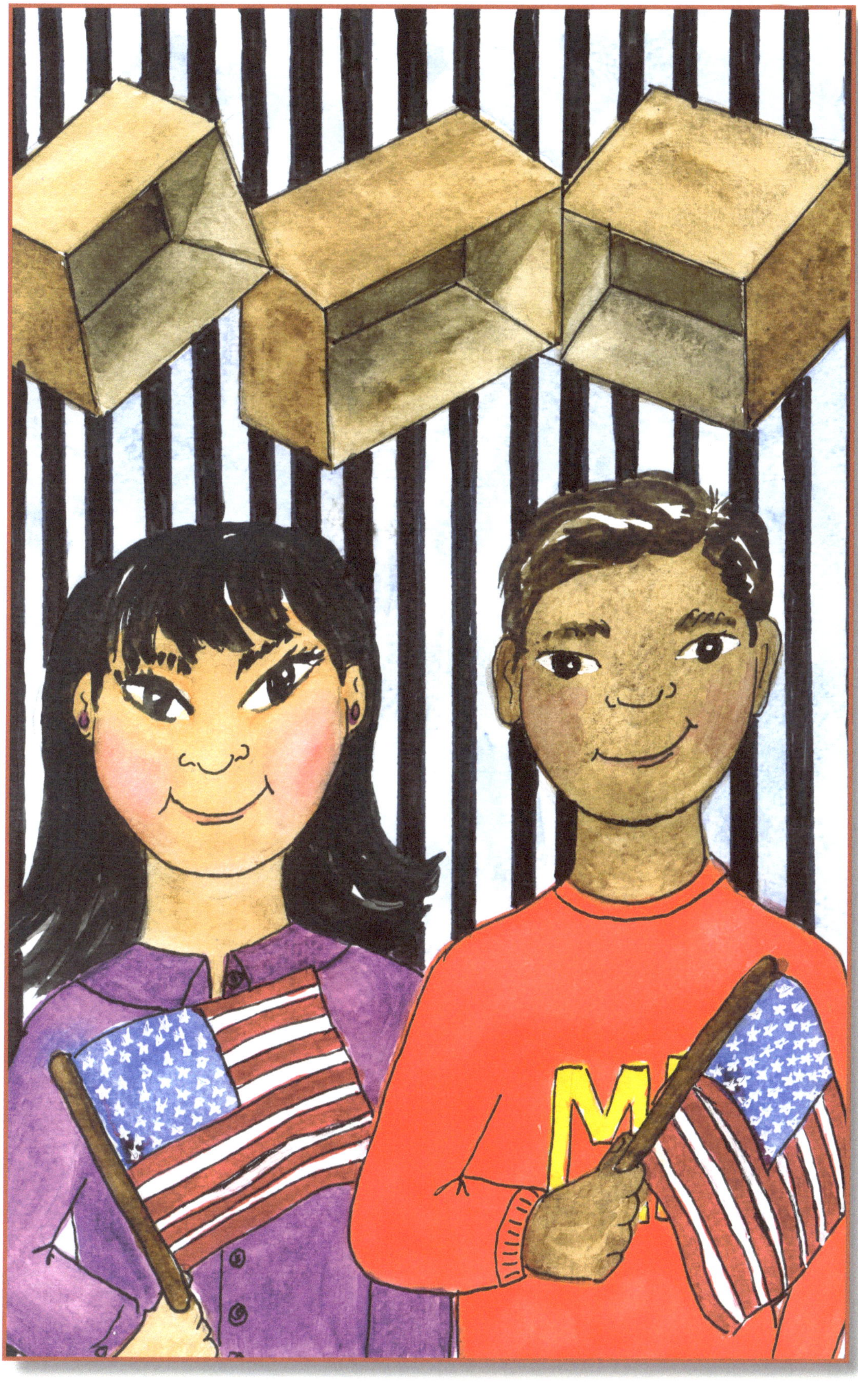

About the Author

Dr. Raj was born and brought up in Mumbai, India and came to Dallas, TX after his medical degree to pursue a doctoral degree in Immunology at the University of Texas Southwestern Medical Center. After a surgical fellowship at Johns Hopkins Hospital in Baltimore he has spent over two decades at the Washington University School of Medicine as an educator, researcher, surgeon, and scientist. He and his wife met in Dallas and currently live in St. Louis, Missouri with their two boys. This is his first book.

About the Illustrator

Jean McMullen is an artist/illustrator/teacher/gallery owner. She graduated from Southern Illinois University with a Masters in Secondary Art Education. Jean taught Art in the public schools for 25 years and presently owns and teaches watercolor at Missouri Artists On Main in St. Charles, Missouri. Jean's watercolors are found in many private and public collections nationally and internationally. She enjoys illustrating children's books and always looks forward to each challenge a new story brings. Visit Jean's website at www.jmcmullenart.com.

Milton Keynes UK
Ingram Content Group UK Ltd.
UKHW050621301124
451951UK00009B/71